Middens of the Tribe

Other Books by Daniel Hoffman

Poetry

An Armada of Thirty Whales
A Little Geste
The City of Satisfactions
Broken Laws
Striking the Stones
The Center of Attention
Able Was I Ere I Saw Elba
Brotherly Love
Hang-Gliding from Helicon

Criticism

Paul Bunyan, Last of the Frontier Demigods
The Poetry of Stephen Crane
Form and Fable in American Fiction
Barbarous Knowledge
Poe Poe Poe Poe Poe Poe Poe
Faulkner's Country Matters
Words to Create a World

As Editor

The Red Badge of Courage and Other Tales
American Poetry and Poetics
Harvard Guide to Contemporary American Writing
Ezra Pound & William Carlos Williams

Middens of the Tribe

A Poem by Daniel Hoffman

Louisiana State University Press
Baton Rouge and London

1995

Copyright © 1978, 1995 by Daniel Hoffman
Manufactured in the United States of America
First printing
04 03 02 01 00 99 98 97 96 95   5 4 3 2 1

Designer: Glynnis Phoebe
Typeface: Bembo
Typesetter: Moran Printing, Inc.
Printer and binder: Thomson-Shore, Inc.

Library of Congress Cataloging-in-Publication Data
Hoffman, Daniel, 1923–
        Middens of the tribe : a poem / by Daniel Hoffman.
            p.   cm.
        ISBN 0-8071-2000-6 (cl). — ISBN 0-8071-2001-4 (p)
        I. Title.
        PS3515.02416M53   1995
        811'.54—dc20   94-46351
                                                                          CIP

Section 19 appeared under the title "Haunted Houses" in the March, 1978, issue of *Poetry.*

The paper in this book meets the guidelines for permanence and durability of the Committee on Pro-
duction Guidelines for Book Longevity of the Council on Library Resources. ∞

Middens of the Tribe

Listen. You'll overhear neither the
living, nor the dying, nor the dead
each of whom hoards dreams that he cannot
tell anybody, and cannot keep
from watching happen in his head. They'll
confide in you—you'll keep their secrets?

1

While his wife, who is consoled by Faith, is praying,
  making offerings, and otherwise preparing
    for Life after Death, with his black
      satchel he makes house calls.

He never goes out without his satchel, or without
  leaving with his answering service the numbers
    of all the houses he will visit,
      for all his house calls

pursue him. No sooner has he arrived at a house attending
  a father who, laid off at the railroad yard,
    had spent two nights and two days wasting
      his severance pay in taprooms

and, getting into a fight at a bar, was brought home bleeding
  from welts, with bruises and a broken nose,
    unable to pay for his wife and five
      children's next meal, much less

a doctor's fee, than the physician, while bandaging him
  pro bono, is rung up and summoned to the other
    side of town. There, in a brownstone
      house the buzzer lets him

open the door, and, mounting the stairs, he'd find the boy
  of only five, dying of meningitis.
    His satchel holds no palliative
      to cool that forehead, no

unguent to soothe the throat through which faint breath,
  rasping, scarcely trickled as the boy
    moaned behind glazed eyes. Coming
      down the street, on his way

to call on the old man who lived by himself in a mansion
hung with large paintings of cows in bosky
glens and of a naked woman
bathing and being watched

by an old man at the window of a large house containing
pictures of cattle fording a stream and women
undraped and bathing, he would be
spotted while getting out

of the taxi—someone would see his satchel and call out:
Doctor, Doctor, this way! There's been a terrible
accident—he'd follow the breathless
fellow to the corner where

a young woman lay sprawled on the cobbles next the car tracks,
a dark trickle stretching itself in the grooves
between the stones beneath her head.
There, he'd kneel down,

take out his gold pocket watch, pick up her wrist,
then let it fall. Up in the tapestried
bedroom of the old man
whom he called on twice

a week, and whose complaint, the debility of age,
he could not stanch, he'd prescribe a water
pill, a change of sleeping pill,
and another antidepressant,

a laxative with fresher taste and the butler would say,
Sir, it's your office on the phone, and he would
take the message, pack his satchel,
and go to the rooming house

downtown where the birth was expected. This time the labor
was premature, the infant's head already
emerging by the time he'd washed
his hands—

                    Is it going well?

the father calls from behind the door, but the doctor
　　does not reply, for by now the birth has fallen
　　　　into the light—as the mother moans
　　　　　　her relief at the loss

of heaviness in her womb, the pain already subsiding
　　in her loins, the doctor holds the neckless
　　　　stillborn fetus, head like a frog's
　　　　　　and the hands like flippers

with twigs for legs, what the age before our knowledgeable
　　age would have called a monstrous birth
　　　　and the mother with her long blonde
　　　　　　hair would have been hanged

for a witch, but now he must think of something to say
　　to the parents. It's been a hard day.
　　　　The doctor is glad to return home
　　　　　　at last, to loosen his tie

and sit him down at his own table for a good
　　supper and a glass of wine. And now
　　　　his wife is lighting the candles. Next,
　　　　　　she'll ask him to say the blessing.

2

The litany of their names sustained him.

The noble numbers of that nomenclature summoned the titans and the heroes, the outsized, triumphant corporate bodies whose offices occupied entire floors of downtown skyscrapers, whose executives were domiciled therein with private, ample, many-windowed chambers looking out from upper stories upon the widespread bustling world invisibly governed from the buzzer-buttons and telephones upon their desks. Here was the heart of life itself, the concentration of energy and purpose that made possible the growth of portfolios, the expansion of holdings, conglomeration of industries, rises in brackets, capital gains.

Peabody, Proskauer, Leibowitz & Smith
Duffield Noonan Duffield
D'Aubigny Frères
Corcoran, Walker, Fitch & Kahn

And there was the swifter inventory of acronyms and numerals emitting with the crackle of a firing range from the dome-shaped ticker, the endless tape unspooling through his hands as its telegraphic messages impelled it—

GM $60\frac{1}{4}$ . . . ITT 132 . . . READING RWY 134 . . . SCOTT 61 . . . DUPONT $170\frac{1}{4}$ . . . AETNA 232 . . .

These ever-changing symbols and figures on their ribbon in curls upon the floor signified, by their jagged upward progression, the basic soundness of the nation. He who held this ribbon in his hands, understanding full well the cycles of expansion and their technical corrections, thus possessing the knowledge of free markets and their innate laws by which to avail himself of the system's unending largesse, could feel, as the figures rose, that he had merged his destiny with that of his country and his time.

How often, chair-ridden now, he relived those vibrant days. Then, if ever, the richness of life, the fullness of energy had arisen within him and lifted him to the heights of daring and of being. Never so with his wife; her great gift was knowing just the moment to cut him down, her tongue never lacking the barb to puncture the cloud of his confidence, his self-esteem. Nor had he felt so powerful even with— what was her name, why can't he remember? the waitress—who, perhaps because only an ignorant girl, though ardent and pretty, and knowing enough to coax him along then when he was not in his youth any more—not even with her had he felt that surge of power, the significance of being himself, the identity of his desire with his destiny.

The roll call of great brokerage houses echoes, their names reverberating in a windowless vault behind steel grilles. Certain days he recalls, summons back again and again, when Consolidated Ventures broke 235, when Intertemp Preferred attained 178½, and he, foretelling the downswing like the old salt who steered by the taste of the brine, sold before the break. Ah, to breathe the air of those days once again, to have again the minions of Peabody, Proskauer on call to do his bidding. But now there's only one name he calls, 'Charles!' who comes not soon enough to do his bidding—'*Charles!*' What boots it that the Financial District once had served his will, now that he must summon help to pee. '*Charles!*'

3

How could there have been another woman?

4

You look at this old man and what do you see? A poor old geezer who has to piss in a pot every ten minutes, can't sleep nights, takes two and a half hours every morning to move his bowels. Here, after I've brought his lap rug and tucked him up, he sits in his big chair, looking out the window.

He's surrounded himself in this house with the finest things, works of art, silver epergnes, marble columns, urns brought back from Italy, curtains and tapestries from France, and paintings. He was the most careful purchaser of paintings, spent hours in the galleries, consulted the auctioneer and the curator at the Museum. Really knew what he was doing.

Take that one upstairs, you look at it, and what do you see? A life-like painting of a bunch of cows. Right? But he paid $25,000 for that. A smart investment, that's what. The art market is beyond the likes of you or me, but you can take my word the demand for this sort of bucolic realism is bound to rise.

And you've seen that other one, the Biblical scene, painted with exquisite care, every detail just as real as can be. Why, you can even see the nipples on Susanna peeking though her fingers clasped across her breasts. There's never going to be less of a market for religious art.

Susanna and the Elders—I don't mind looking at that one myself. But he doesn't look at it any more. Doesn't look at anything. Would you think, to see him, that he's worth maybe a million? Maybe more. And nobody comes to see him.

Fact is, except for you calling on me here in the kitchen, there's nobody in this house for weeks on end but him and me and Cook, and, on Tuesdays and Fridays, the doctor. You might well think, with all that money waiting for them, they would come.

But his daughter hasn't spoken to him, not a word in fifteen years. Won't even send a card at Christmas. And his sons are too busy to be any comfort to him, the one running the firm downtown, the other digging bones in Yucatán or Wales. So there's no comfort for him, just the empty waiting.

He used to read the papers, then he'd need a hand lens to find the stock prices in the small print; now he gets the paper but it just lies there on his lap. He used to like fine food—lobster thermidor, French sauces, wines—what a wine cellar he has downstairs!

But it's been at least two years now since he had me open a Clos de Vougeot '27, and he didn't drink but half a glass of that. Don't I wish he'd call me to uncork another one of those—someone has to finish the opened wine . . .

Oh no, I'd never think of abusing his trust concerning the wine cellar. How do you think I've held this post for nearly thirty years while all the rest of the staff changed about as often as the Royal Guard in London? You've never seen the changing of the Guard? Well, that's been one of the advantages of this position, the foreign travel.

But how he just sits in his chair, and dozes. Except when he rings the bell or calls so I can fetch him to the toilet. Which he does about every ten minutes or so. In truth, he hasn't got much to look forward to.

I think he waits now for the only thing that can happen to him. And so do I, for I think to myself, when it's over and done, I know what, after thirty years, is in the cards for me. Foreign travel, Clos de Vougeot, the like of that. All the advantages.

5

He really needed her, for all the times he'd tried
to do 'La Baigneuse' from memory, although
he'd get the outline downright perfect, the skin tones
never quite came clear—without the sunlight
pouring on her, he couldn't seem to match
the ruddy, high coloration of the shoulders
and those thighs; the creaminess of the breasts
were skimmed milk unless he had her there
before him. And why was that, he wondered? Memory,
invention, the inwardness of vision in
his work, seascapes with grizzled boulders slashed
by tongues of dark water, the tidal pools
that he made glitter as in his mind, crags
topped by spruces jutting sawtoothed silhouettes
into a sky of abysmal blackness—
all these private fantastications, now stacked
face against the wall in his closet, drew
from him all visionary power. Unsalable.
Carstairs had all but thrown him out the door.
Margate wouldn't touch them. At Kimberton Galleries
a grave though sympathetic shaking of the head
and a word to the wise: You have all sorts of skill,
why don't you paint for us what we can sell, and
for yourself paint what you like. Hence, now,
the sixth in his series requiring exactest reproduction
of her bulging, overweighted flesh with its Tuscan coloration,
the tint of tits and pointed nipples and the hair coiled
just so, fetchingly, about the ear—why, what is he being
but a pimp with a paintbrush—a pornographer whose work,
seen in the houses of the rich, is therefore respectable. There,
that pose is just about perfect, and now this touch and
this, to make her image on the canvas even
more provocative than she is before him. And
he can't deny that in her plump fashion she really is
rather arousing. Now then, he can let her dress

until after supper, when they'll both undress—but
meantime he'll sketch in the rest of the scene. Where
is that *Scribner's* with the illustrations
of Biblical costumes? Even
Rembrandt had to live. Besides, she makes
the best spaghetti since his student year in Rome.
Seeing her move about the cluttered studio in her shift,
those great curves he had spent the afternoon replicating in color
only half outlined beneath the fabric, he grows impatient
for the coming of the night.

6

How could he have kept another woman?
How, when in his heart, his mind, his tiny imagination
he had no room for any mistress but the one
who ruled his life . . . ?

7

Tall black stacks. The ship all white. On the life-ring
in gold outlined with red, SS PERDU.
Brisk breeze. At last, at last, he'll soon be sailing
on his own, the whole trip his affair, nobody
else's business where he goes. Elbowed by strangers
at the rail, waving to the throngs lining the pier,
white handkerchiefs fluttering, then in unison
swaying back and forth. Flags dip. Glitter on the water.
There, waving among the rest, he sees his father,
already farther off, small among the crowd,
and as a sailor casts the hawser off, the liner's horn
shakes the sky with roars, with roars, with roars,
the pier recedes and father shrinks, shrinks,
no bigger than a cricket waving handkerchief as
he sets sail alone. Turning,
the deck's deserted, derrick swaying idly as the tramp
wallows in a swell. Where is the deckhand
with his baggage? The purser? He grabs the rail,
inches toward the life-ring, SS PERDIEM, lurches
over littered deck to bulkhead, through
swinging door to dingy corridor. His pocket!
Wallet's gone!—he has no ticket then. Men
in sailor suits wearing fedoras press
past him in the narrow hall. One bare bulb
on twisted cord sways toward the lurching wall.
Where is he going? Belowdecks, vibration
of the engine and the screw. There's
an officer, braided cuffs, boards on his shoulder
—'Sir!' he cries, 'Captain!'—who pauses
in the stairwell's shadow, half turns to say
'Just leave all operations in my hands.'
He follows after, running up the stairs, the catwalk,
follows as the officer with *Barron's*
and a pigskin briefcase in his hands
strides to the bridge. 'The way I made

sure my ship comes in,' his father's saying
into the phone, hand cupped so no one else can hear,
'is mastering every detail of the business.
No one but you,' with a wink of lighthouse eye,
'will take it over, because nobody else
will run it as I want it run.' The ship's name, carved
on a gilded plaque beneath the window of the bridge, is
SS PADRE, and the hold is full.

8

Hopes centered on his firstborn namesake, Father
added '& Son' to make the firm dynastic.
Though Junior writhes at the confinements of life
there, he can't summon up the guts to defy
our father's wishes. Sis defies his wishes,
though. Apple of his eye, won't come near enough
to let his eye again behold her . . . Mother
meanwhile had eyes only for her baby. Me.
With love like the sweet sap that, poured around a
scarab, congeals, she needed Baby. Amber
stiffened Baby to the amulet she'd wear,
her immortality in the very shape
she's made herself. That poor beetle had no chance
to shape up on his own there. Can the middens
of the tribe I study tell if family
strife always reveals a culture's dynamics,
if, amid bones, flints, sufferings are the same?

9

How could there have been another woman?
How, when in his tiny imagination
he had room for one mistress only,
the one who ruled his life. . . . In bed beside him,
while his teeth ground, I'd hear the ticker
coiled in his brain spit out the tape—Oh, there
was 'evidence,' a witness Dawson found to swear
she'd seen him enter, then leave a flat he paid
the rent for under an assumed name. There,
she said, he kept his woman. So much for truth
in divorce actions, so long as I was freed.
Grounds enough in incompatibility, in mental
cruelty, but no, Dawson has to earn his fee
and make it airtight. But I'm the one
who knew him through and through and truly knew
he had but one romance. For him to be,
by morning, a sudden millionaire, *that* was
romance. All it required was revolt in Venezuela,
civilians to throw the Junta out, and then
that killing he made in Barranquilla Copper
at 3¼ per share would soar to thirty, forty. . . .
Meanwhile, their value hovers between 2
and 3 cents on the dollar while he holds
our 90,000 shares. On how many such
solid ventures, investment risks, wild geese
he frittered my money away, I never knew.
These were his rites of worship to his mistress,
the Market, whom he'd propitiate
like a goddess. She got our every cent.
Why, there were months I couldn't pay Gristede's,
months we had nothing, and when a hunch paid off
he still was close, his gains plunged in 'investment.'
A big spender like that would pay the rent
or buy baubles under an assumed name for a tart?
How could he have kept another woman!

10

Evidence suggests there was among them a
cult of shamans, priesthood of the powerful.
Although all life among the Cromlech People
is traditional, the hereditary
chieftainship descending on the mother's side,
these they choose by rendering their dreams. *E.g.,*
'While others slept I alone saw her. First Bear
strode across the August sky. There, where she walked,
a brilliant falling star seared a white archway
seeking his own place to shine in among stars
who guard their tents. But when he came near First Bear,
mother of stars, she ate him and the sky paled.
The Great Spirit moved these figures in my eyes
that look inward. I stand on the cliff most near
Grandfather Sun, Grandmother Moon. My hands hold
no sling, no spear, in my mouth no food until
I shall touch and grasp the power of my dream.'

11

He has no daughter. Sons, he has two sons, one a diminution
of himself who bumbles the business he had built toward ruin,
the other a wise fool, off in Wales or Arizona digging
dead men's bones. But bitter, bitter, nothing
more so in the disappointments, losses, the betrayals
of a lifetime, than her rejection. She
must have drawn her spite in with her mother's milk,
for where could she have learned to scorn him so
but from the one whose curdled heart has poured
these years of venom and abuse on him? What else
could turn the obedient pretty child that he begot,
now grown into a woman, savage,
because to fill the aching place his wife's contempt
left void and dry, he had but asked of her
a daughter's love, the affection that is owed
a father, he who, when she was a babe in arms
had, from the bath, lifted her in his arms
and drenched her still-damp nape with kisses . . . You
who crouched, invisible to all but him,
at her birth on the head of her cradle, what would you say
is such a daughter's portion, one whose scorn
drops poison daily in his memory's cup?
One drop of the dark fluid from your sagging breast
squeezed on the pool and look, the fish turn
belly-up, and now you'd squeeze a drop in
her martini—what an idea!—he stands
invisible, inanimate, as on a film
spun through his brain he watches, sees, he does
nothing, makes no move, says nothing, while
Daughter lifts the glass, turns ashen, moans,
clutches her stomach, stumbles, writhing, falls . . .
Cora! the child is ill! he calls, his wife
picks up the four-year-old and soothes her down
on the couch, *Call the doctor, fool! Why don't*
you call the doctor? His bloated fingers stub

the dial, misdial, he dials again, the dial
moves O so slowly till the busy buzz
burrs in his ear, he dials again, he hears
a distant voice, The doctor is on call . . .
So smart you'd be the copper king of Wall Street
don't sit there helpless, drive the child
to the hospital yourself! She lays his daughter down
on the back seat of the Studebaker
with fenders flared like a Stutz Bearcat's and optional
freewheeling. The starter whirrs, the engine
coughs, coughs, dry-coughs, coughs—*You idiot*
she cries, *you've let the tank go dry again,*
and now, in the dark, he must set out to fetch
some gas without a gas can, so, from the stoop
he'll take the empties left for Sheffield Farms
and runs, runs down the windy street, his arms
clutching a box of milk bottles until
at an intersection, under one glum bulb
a SINCLAIR dinosaur swings from a pole
and a greasy wizened man who looks like him
feeds the spout into his bottle, turns
the handcrank and the pointer slowly sweeps
around the dial slowly, as fumes rise
and liquid swishes in the glass. Returned,
he lifts the glass, pours quart and quart
into the tank, now turns the key, it takes, he's
speeding through the rain the wipers
sweeping momentary clearness skidding
around turns, there's the sign
EMERGENCY and swoops, braking
to a stop. No light, door closed. He knocks.
Rattles doorjamb. Silence like a pulse beats loud.
Kicks the door. Peers through dirty pane.
Inside is dark. A passerby
calls, Don't you know it's closed? They moved
to Whitewood over a year ago. Now
he, drenched, grasps steering wheel again and
drives pellmell again through lights, red lights,
crossings, railroad tracks, and comes

in the suburbs to the rolling drive that leads
to illuminated sign URGENCY and
leaps, engine running, through the door—My
daughter's dying! he cries, but the cheese-faced
woman in white dress with pencil on a string
tied to her clipboard demands to see his card
—His card?—Medical Insurance Card before
a patient is admitted here. He reaches
for his wallet—pocket empty! In the rush
to call the doctor, start the car, get the gas,
find the hospital, he's left his wallet
home, on bedside table . . . Without a card
the hospital requires cash in advance
she says. But with no wallet how can he have cash
and his daughter's terribly sick, a child in pain,
she must be seen at once by doctor—there, there's
a doctor—Doctor, my daughter's in the car,
she's sick, and this white cow who's spiteful as my wife
won't admit the child. You are a doctor,
you took the Hippocratic oath, for God's
sake, I'll pay you later, look at her—Doctor
grasps the car doorhandle, flings it wide,
peers in, and says The seat is empty.
You have no daughter.

12

The light was aglow with the blueness of the sea, the tingles of sea-
mist gathered into the wind as it passed outlying islands and
crossed the shingle of the cove,

then climbed the steep turf field strewn with grey boulders, until,
passing over the plastered chimney and thatched roof of his fa-
ther's cottage, the wind with its armload of mist dipped in the
blue of the sea

sped up the mountain and thence into the vast sky where clouds were
already piled in pearly baskets. He flung open the door and gazed
down

on the pasturage where their sheep nuzzled sparse grass, emitting
bleats and baaas that came flickering on the wind. Across the
stony road

stretched the beach, and in the crook of the sandspit reeds swayed and
rose, rose and bowed, as the breeze, now declined to a cat's-paw,
played amongst them.

He ran down the hill to the shore, past the thickets that hid the dark
entrance to the cave where blessed Father Mulcahy had said the
Mass in secret, on down the shingle, skipping between

the standing stones of the cromlechs where the pagan warriors bowed
to their ancient gods. As he stood by the brink of the water, he
could see

the curlews flash above him, and then, suddenly, as though gathered
out of the mist, the approaching wedge of a skein of barnacle
geese

honking their goose-talk as they circled in for a landing: A roar of

wings, splash of water, and they were down, hardly visible
amongst the reeds. He picked up from the beach

a round stone to fling it out—not to hit them, he wouldn't dare risk
killing a flyer from behind the North Wind whose bird-body
contained a soul

condemned, for not receiving the sacraments, to fly about the world
forever until the Day of Judgment—but just to get the geese

to take off and fly, he so loved the roar of their wings as they buffeted
the water into froth and beat the air until it foamed and held
their hugh bodies aloft—There!

he spun his stone seaward in a looping arc, it dipped among the reeds,
then made a muffled splash and the sky trembled to the roar of
the great seabirds straining

wild pinions in the blue light—they beat, they beat, and beat the wa-
ter among the reeds, then the many-winged skein of geese arose,
beating and honking,

all but the one bird lamely, pitifully thrashing a dozen yards from shore,
flailing its one good wing against the broken reeds, trailing

across its back the grotesquely extended other wing that in his heart
a lump as heavy and indigestible as a sob of grief told him he

unwittingly had hit with his ill-flung stone. As the flock came roar-
ing and honking over his head, by their sounds attempting to re-
trieve their fallen brother and take him along

as they glided on toward purer, higher, bluer air across the bay, the El-
evated train roars past his window, rousing him to breathe

old rancid cooking smells. Dead cabbages. Cold grease. Eileen, in her
wrapper, opens and closes the icebox door, a rasher of bacon for
his breakfast. The kids

are already squabbling in the next room. Beneath his bed, like battle

casualties, workboots sprawl. As he sits up, stretches in the grimy
air and buttons his shirt,

he looks at the clock on the dresser. Just time to bolt his breakfast,
seize his lunch pail, catch the El to the railroad works, where his
day will pass

in the gloom of the locomotive shed and the glare of lanterns, the air
heavy and tired with the weight of smoke and oil, the din of en-
gines, drills, jackhammers, coupling cars.

13

The climax of the act of course is sawing
a woman in half. The old illusionist returns
onstage, doffs his top hat, bows gravely to the audience
as two young lady assistants appear from the wings,
they, too, in white bow ties, top hats, and tails,
but wearing skimpy black panties, sleek white stockings, and high
   heels.
As the applause dies down they cross the stage
and wheel in, on a sort of trolley, a long wooden box.
Then, in his most portentous tone, the magician asks,
Is there among us tonight anyone willing
to be sawn in half?
             A deep gasp
circles the balconies and boxes. There is a pall
of silence. At last, in the second row, a lovely girl
with long hair and a sleek figure raises her hand. She seems
tentative, a little afraid, perhaps, but then, with faltering
resolve, as of one who has taken a dare from the friend beside her,
who, should she now renege, will tease her the rest of the evening,
comes forward.
              The ladies in tights descend to meet her.
A spotlight picks her out as they climb onstage. A very
photogenic miss, with her bare shoulders
beneath the flowing golden hair, her slender
waist and tapering legs. The magician assures the audience
'She won't feel a thing, all she need do is
climb into this box'—she is standing behind it—and
he lowers the lid
so her head protrudes from a hole at one end,
feet from holes at the other. The young ladies
in tights, high heels, and top hats take their places
at either end—the drum rolls—
                The magician grasps his saw
firmly, raises one foot to the box, and leans
into his work. The rip of saw against the wood makes

harsh shrieking sounds. Sawdust flies in a cloud,
dimming the footlights. It sure looks
like he's cutting that girl in half! Now
she seems agitated, is saying something to him, perhaps
protesting that she doesn't any longer wish to be
sawn in half tonight, but we cannot
hear her voice over the rasp of the bucksaw.
What's this? Has
something gone wrong? The attendant ladies rush forward, then
bending over the sawn box, pull
the halves apart—

        By God, he's done it, he has
cut the young lady in two!

                —on their high heels wheel the two parts
of the box offstage amid applause. But look!—
coming out from the flaps, can it be
the girl we just saw sawn in half?
Yes, it's her! She walks into the spotlight, her golden hair
gleams on her white shoulders, and now
she smiles, she blows kisses to the audience cheering
her miraculous deliverance from the teeth
of the saw of Dr. Magic.

             Tomorrow
the show will go on again, at the same time,
the illusionist will again ask for a volunteer from the audience
and once more there will be gasps, and a pause. And then,
in the second row, a spotlight will whiten an upraised hand.
Whose will it be?—the light catches
her white arm, her long blonde hair!
His attendants in tights will descend to escort her
again to the footlights and the show
continues as he blows on the teeth of the saw
expectantly, while they lift her into the box. The audience
sucks in its breath, awaiting
the climax of the act—

14

The simple transactions—shopping for bread, for cheese, for a bottle
of milk and the morning paper—these you can do well enough,
with hardly a trace of a wheeze.

But just let you try saying *Good morning* to a pretty girl in the hall
while you think *What a passionate face! My God, what a pair!*
then it all comes out in a sneeze.

If at the office you're asked, Where are those letters you filed last
night? or I've got to reach the top shelf, will you help me up on
this stool?

it's the same as when you were called on in class or heard your cue
in the Christmas play at school.

You dare not leave your room but your pockets are stuffed with
Kleenex. You love

watching TV, so much conversation and you never are called on to
answer. It's a life

like the life you'd live if you could; but fatherhood, marriage, a pro-
posal, even a pickup, a lay

are out of the question. You'd be all right, you'd be fine

if living were dumbshow. Or if you could learn to speak up

without having to breathe. Then the sun would float at high noon on
the tide of your words, and your feelings would flood the coun-
ters and lintels and beds of the world as you'd speak, and speak
firm, impassioned, assured—

All of your words are ready.

15

Did I tell that sonofabitch? Did I tell him?

You can bet your sweet patootie I told him where to shove his
  thumb and when he got it out to chew it, lousy bastard

standing there in his neat coat, white collar like he stole it out of a
  Arrow ad, his thin black tie

around his neck—I'd like to strung him up on his thin black tie,

standing there in his little black shiny patent leather shoes

telling me I'm sorry he says, may his tongue fall out for saying it,
  I'm sorry

to have to give you this pink slip Mister Brophy he says, we are
  compelled by circumstances

beyond our control to reduce the force in the roundhouse. Circum-
  stances beyond our control my ass,

he always had it in for me. Never liked me. And you wanna know
  why?

Did he have a better man on the day shift in the roundhouse?

Did he? You ever overhauled a locomotive? I can tell you, Buster,

it's a man's job. But he gave me the slip. Never liked me

since that roundhouse picnic in the park last Labor Day

when his wife—she is a *dish*—she was all over me behind the
  boathouse.

I mean, was it my fault his wife was all over me there on the picnic?

That pastyfaced bastard in the office who don't know a piston from
  his own pecker,

he wouldn't know how to couple a cab to an engine, much less
  couple himself, if you take me.

Circumstances beyond his control, and how the hell am I supposed
  to feed my wife and five kids?

Did I tell you we have five kids?—there's James, and Kevin, and
  Mary Elizabeth

and Nora. What do you mean, only four? Well there's Johnny Ju-
  nior ain't there? What about him?

So this husband of hers keeps his grudge bleeding like a running
  sore till he can give me the pink

circumstances beyond his control—And to whom might I be refer-
  ring to?

Why who the hell do you think I'm referring to?—Mister George
   Wilson,
supervisor of the railroad roundhouse and first-class prick. And what's
   that to you?
Yeah? I don't give a fart if he is your brother-in-law, he's a little tin-
   cock emperor and you can tell the twit I

16

Characteristic of the Cromlech People
is the evident arrangement of their tombs,
the sons beside their fathers and grandfathers,
each with tools in flint or bone of the same trade.
We find no evidence of adolescent
rebellion against the ascription of fixed
roles. Yet what society can last without
providing mechanisms for expressing
revolt, subsumed, perhaps, or sublimated
so the girded structure of institutions
remains intact? Where do the Cromlechs sanction
expression of those anarchic energies
the individual may purge himself of
yet not rend the web that their society
has woven round him? Look, my instincts told me,
for verses scribed upon their funeral urns,
their buried flutes, look to the walls of their caves.

17

Awaking after after-sleep, he climbed
out of the bed and went naked to the toilet to pee.
A shaft of pallor dropped through the skylight on the bed.
He got back in without disturbing her, pulling the sheet,
then pressed his knees inside the warm bends of her knees,
his hip against the soft mound of her buttock, and flung
his arm around her elbow, resting his hand upon her breast.
In the spent moonlight his eyes closed on a scene that he,
half waking, half asleep, knew that he knew
as he wittingly dreamed of the perfect harmony
the violent thrashing of their bodies had, as they subsided,
spread upon the obliterated night.

The center was a golden surging, a crest uprising
from wild tongues of flame consuming particles of black
and violet that whirled in their inexorable conjunctions,
thousands of tiny pairs linked to each other by bonds
that joined them each to each yet held each one apart.
From the chaos of individuated specks the size of atoms, linked
into pairs yet the pairs not melding into single wholes, from all
that frustrated energy of half-fulfillment came
the discharge of the spectrum radiating upward in a jet
of self-consuming flame, an intensity that devours
its own smoke, its own mass, till all its properties
are a radiance so bright the eye can scarce endure it.
This he would paint, or strive to paint, henceforth;
no more the literal depiction of her body merely, for how
could that express the reality of love? They had become,
by virtue of consciously not thinking on it, reconciled
to pandering his admiration of her beauty
to indulge the fantasies of grosser men. Knowing her
as he knew her, he'd be content no more
with tones of flesh or the inviting gestures
of her hands. His paintings would give homage
to the power of Woman, the immortal energy

that called from him this glimpse of pure emotion,
as best his brush might try to hold that evanescent power
beyond the mere appearance of their selves.

18

The day we moved into that ugly house
with French windows in every room, I promised
to decorate it in a manner fit
for my successful husband. Within a month
I saw him, dumbstruck, shuffle up the walk
between our blazing maples that black day,
the 29th, a beaten man, so ruined
we couldn't pay for curtains. And yet
by Christmas wasn't he again outwitting
his mistress with one of those systems which
comprised his articles of belief?—each learned
from books by mail with a coupon clipped from *Barron's*
and a check for forty dollars. Schemes to interpret
highs and lows against the swings in rainfall
in the corn and wheat belts. Or predicting
how every seven years Dow Jones Industrials
are swayed by the precessions of the moon. A man
obsessed by intellectual pursuits has neither
the need, the time, nor room in his imagination
to set up apartments for a floozie. Nor
had he any notion of what it means
—or could have meant—to have a wife, a woman
to whom he might have shown a little attention,
much less love. I speak of love no longer;
once married, I never again found on the doorstep
a delivery boy with a florist's box for me.
Life with him was a plot of cactus. No
oasis, no companionship, affection.
No room for passion save his crazy hunches,
plays on tips from brokers' sycophants,
anyone with a rumor from the Street caught
his heartstrings by the hand. He had no room
in the cubicle of his imagination crammed
with closing prices and predicted trends,
to rent a flat, to keep another woman.

19

Jimbo Johnson mocked and Fu Bigonzi dared me,
Waiting at the gate end of the weedy walk
For me to prove they lied. So at each further step
Through burrs and blazing goldenrod, retreat became
Unlikelier. I climbed the trellis up the porch
Pretending it was any trellis, any porch,
And snaked across the peeling shingles to the window
Where one board was split. I pulled that board ajar
And leaning upward, pried the window open. Then,
With a clear way awaiting me, the slanting sun
Throbbed on the porch roof heat that pulsed as my head pulsed.
I turned, to turn back down the tindery splintered shingles,
Shimmy down the raingutter and fall in a shower
Of rust on blistered hands to the crushed cool grass
—Taunted a quitter?—Iron-breath'd, I climbed in
One leg, both legs, dropped then into the murky coolness
On the landing of the stairs: Below, in half-light
Needles of light, their eyes knotholes in the boarded windows,
Sewed light-seams slantwise toward the shadowed floor.
I gripped the banister, dislodged a shower of dust
That fell and rose and swirled along the five sunbeams.
I took a slow step down. A mahogany table still
Held two ceramic paperweights upon a pile
Of letters someone had received and had not answered.
A look of life half-lived, a table setting still
Awaiting two, two chairs by the ashen log on the firedogs.
Two glasses on the sideboard next the staircase stood,
A dust-stoppered decanter by them, dust and dead
Flies in the glasses. Who had lived together here
Beneath a mica shade where wrought-iron *Niña, Pinta,*
And *Santa María* sail their circles round and round
An unlit globe of glass on dark and dusty seas?
Who left and never have returned to claim their own?
Why don't they come to claim their own,
To live companionable lives out at this hearth ·

For two, table for two, decanter set for two
—Or do they still move here among these mouse-gnawed letters,
Caress familiar furniture with touch that can't
Dislodge one grain of dust in the half-light? As I turned
At the bottom of the stair some silent thing turned toward me,
Raised its arms and shrieked my shriek—pure terror
Slit its frogwhite face with voice I knew and know.
No doubt that bulging china closet's glass bowfront
Had caught grotesque reflections from these stairs before—
But I was skinning down the rainspout when that thought
Found chink to clutch to in the riptide of my fear.
Yet I'd been, and not on dares, in eerier houses
Where one among one of a pair of candelabra,
Six of a dozen goblets, half a set of silver
Kept house where every swelling spoon's a mantic mirror
That makes her huge who sits to table, makes the empty
Facing chair a thin vein 'round the mirror's eyelid;
And another where another's half-dozen of a dozen
Knives, forks, spoons, six of twelve matched goblets
And half a pair of candelabra makes a setting
For a half-life where the absent ghost exacts
A compound interest from this capital, as he
—Inmate of a present no reflection ends—
Exacts like interest whose own penury's the same.
There's an oval glass in either's hallway. I have seen
My hand on the knobs before those mirrors and behind,
Almost proof, you'd think, against all haunting.

20

In this culture, the onset of puberty
marks the entryway to one of the great gates
of life, and, since it is second of the three,
it partakes of both the others. The coming
of sexual maturity is itself
being born again into a new estate,
while this emergence leaves behind, as though dead,
the child one was. Therefore, like their births and deaths,
this is occasion for great ceremony.
All males reaching twelve by the August full moon
spend three days climbing tall cliffs, in foot-races,
in marksmanship with thrown spear, slingshot, and stones.
This is followed by a huge feast the women
have meanwhile been preparing—baked bulrush stems,
bark beakers of fermented cider, roast dog.
Then is each new man led to the threshold of
a leafed bower wherein waits his first woman.

21

Remember when it began?—In the men's shower at the Y, in the
    white tiled cube, rank with the steaming smell of sweat and the
    rancid odor rising from the trough of milky dip at the door

where the feet of every man and boy had to be cleansed of athlete's
    foot. You stood under the warm rain from the nozzle, between
    older men unconcernedly lathering their hairy chests, armpits,
    crotches,

your mind on the mixed swimming and the girls who in school
    were unrevealed in skirts and dresses, even sweaters, standing or
    sitting on the pool's edge with their cleavages, the roundness of
    their arms,

the mounds of their buttocks emerging where scant bathing suits
    hiked up above smooth thighs. You didn't used to notice or care,
    but now this stab in the pit of your stomach, and in your crotch
    a swollen throbbing.

Helplessly you felt your dong grow heavy as a pendulum, then stick
    straight out from its root of several hairs, a pointer pointing. You
    turned to the plain white wall of square tiles dripping

with drops and rivulets, hoping the other guys, who stood in the rush
    of water soaping themselves and singing, hadn't seen, and
    wouldn't see.

You tried to concentrate on the pattern of the tiles, unending squares,
    driblets of water running down. You made your eyes, your
    mind, fasten on those squares, those drops, but your crotch

had other thoughts, your cock swaying with its own inexorable fixa-
    tions. You feel imprisoned in your blood, a flood of shame, with
    the knowing that your mind, your will, are unmanned,

the creatures of your crazed and runaway tool. You reach for the tiller
  of the shower and swing it hard on to COLD—sheets of icy
  needles sting your shoulders, stomach, groin,

you feel your pecker shrivel and balls wither in the harsh grip of frigid
  water. Now you can get into your jock strap. You step into
  your trunks and run for the pool—

Remember?—you dove into the deep end and scissored underwater
  all the way, rising to the surface with lungs bursting, eyes sting-
  ing, breaking out just where, on the ladder,

Betty-Jo was jiggling her bubs as she slowly, shiveringly slithered her
  thighs deeper into the cool green water. 'Hi!' she said, leaning
  her cleavage down

toward you in the water. You'd reply, 'Betty-Jo, you are beautiful,
  looking at you, thinking about you, makes me feel things I never
  felt, I want to touch you, hold you,

just to be near you is a torment and a sweetness I can hardly stand,' but
  while you struggle for the first word your breath catches itself
  coming and going in your throat, you wheeze,

your greeting a grotesque gargle as the fuming chemical water floods
  your mouth, your nose. Betty-Jo is laughing, her head under
  white rubber cap rocking back and forth as her breasts

rise and fall with hilarity, while you, choking with embarrassment,
  with shame, grab the trough at the pool's edge, turn, and shoot
  out toward the deeper water,

eyes stinging from chlorine, tears mingled with cold bubbles in the
  pool.

22

I've got to get out of here. I can't go on
spending every night of my life with my legs
tucked up beneath my chin
inside a wooden box while he
sweats and sways on his bucksaw, charging
through the cardboard—he nearly
nicked my ass last night—as a thousand
gawking fools watch me faking terror,
pretending pain, and think those wooden legs stuck through
the foot of the box with shoes on are mine.
I can't stand this life. And last night,
for the first time, I could see him in the dark
by the light of the neon sign outside the window.
Till now I never knew his face had
the same glazed look I thought he put on in the theatre
when he's sawing me in half. Though he always
did make the same grunts in an undertone
when he fucked as when he sawed. And when I'm not
trapped in a box behind the footlights, I'm in this
hotel room—wherever we are, it's the same
room, the same hotel. And while he spends
hours in the bathroom admiring
himself in the mirror, waxing
his moustache, dousing tonic in his hair, here
am I with my portable iron, leaning
on each of his thirteen colored handkerchiefs,
the black tablecloths, the shawls,
folding them all just so for the act, or pressing
his tails, creasing his trousers, brushing and rebrushing
those three top hats. I wonder if there's a dye
in that tonic, I'm sure he dyes his sideburns. He's a lot
older than he admits. Don't I know he's had
many a girl in that sawbox before
I was fool enough to fall for him?
I *am* a fool. If I ever do get him to the altar, what

would that change? He's had a tumble with the other
girls in the show, I know it, especially
those two, Janeen and Meg, he took along to play Wilkes-Barre.
But I'd better make sure, damned sure, he marries *me*
and soon—I've missed the curse two months now
and it feels like there's somebody curled up with knees
under her chin inside me, waiting to come out.

23

What good's inheriting the company
without a secretary of his own?
Once Doc assured him Father, in Charles's care,
would never leave the house again, right then
he made Dad's old Miss Prill his Business-Minder
Emerita. But who could dream what luck
would send *her* here, first answer to his ad!
At the doorway, when she paused, an exaltation
smote him dumb, yet he trembled with dismay
that instant, knowing she, she is the one
who as a statue steps from its sculptor's mold,
fills an image he hadn't known his mind held.
Then, pulses booming in his temples, voice
croaking from some distant, barbarous cave,
how did he interview her, ascertain
she takes dictation, her typing speed?—at least
she's qualified, so hiring her at once
set off no mutiny in the typing pool. . . .
How get through the week dictating letters
to her crossed legs, her breasts, her hair
tumbling over her shoulders in waves,
pencil at her lips, her lips half-parted
—even the tongue-tied kid in the stockroom stares
as struck by lightning when she saunters past—
Dazed by her presence, he bumbles, soul an ache
of longing, the carpet, wall, window, sky
all one color of incomplete desire
until by the third day, mind a blank, a blank
but for the repetition of her name,
on the interphone, Could she work late tonight?
And by their second drink in the Opal Lounge
he, smitten as he was, could sense
the attraction was, well, reciprocal,
though maybe not, on her part, as intense,
but enough so that next day he leased the flat

(all morning thinking up his alias) for her
('on business, late work, must go out of town')
—Sure beats slinking in and out of motels,
a place to meet in that would be their own.

Outside, the sky is rouged toward twilight
but his mind, empty of the day's concerns,
is bleached but for the echo of her name
while behind that door she types demurely
his correspondence on the day's concerns.
He waits for five, at last the door swings inward
as deferentially she says, Good night,
he says Good night, both quickened by deceit
in this charade before the staff each day.
Even now she's on her way to await him
while he feigns desk work to detain him—best
they go their separate ways to one another.
Turning the fresh-typed letters, his mind sees
them as they were last time, after he'd poured
himself into their wrenching ecstasy,
that wild unsounded violence in his loins
thrust in turbulent harmony and spilt
in the ache of its prolonging, yet in the longing
itself a chill, like fear, wordless foreboding
—What is this guilt that's wedded
to his pleasure in her rapturous moans?—
and then blackout, as flaming tongues arose
enfolding specks of black that whirled behind
his eyes, his mind consumed by radiance, until
all subsides in sleep. And when they rose
and she sat before the mirror to brush her hair
as he knelt beside, a primordial urge to give
homage to her womanhood once more
and kiss her arms, her breasts, her throat—she,
looking at both their faces in the glass, said,
Don't you see, we even look alike. . . .
As he gazed from her reflected brow,
her colleen profile, traced her nose, her chin,
the set of the brows and eyes within that radiant face

to his own image, he saw a coarser version,
masculine, almost brutal, of her grace.
His head rings with a half-stifled acknowledgment,
How strange he hadn't thought . . . hadn't let himself
. . . And so, she said, we must
be destined for each other. Yes, Yes,
that's it. That's it. And now,
in half an hour he'll be again with
Wilma, Wilma, Wilma, Wilma, Wilma,

24

Marriage. No counterpart exists among them
to infatuation, courtship, romantic
love as we conceive love, nor marriage arranged
to pass on tribal rank or wealth. A couple
is drawn together by a power greater
than the tribe possesses. This they must express
as do the spirits, their totem animals.
The coupling of boy and girl, woman and man
shivers with the gift that drives the seasons round.
Joined thus, they are indissoluble for life.
Their sexual pleasure releases them to
the rejoicings spawned tadpoles stir in still ponds,
they subside then to rest like nesting seahawks:
Later, the hatching of the young, the struggles
for food, for space to live, for power, for mates.

25

How, from all the men in the world, did I choose
that one obsessed by the nothingness of life,
a man without interests, without love,
without culture? I tried to bring him
to the theatre, but after four first nights
at the Theatre Guild with Helen Hayes, with Gielgud
on stage and him snoring in his seat
gave up on that. Tried concerts—how bring to music
a donkey with tin ears who couldn't tell
Brahms from Irving Berlin? His one concern
in the arts was Art—of course, blue-chip investments:
filled the house with hideous oversized
canvases by unknown Bulgarians waiting
for Kimberton's to discover their costumed bargirls,
their naked waitresses poised against a background
of Biblical beards. And the sentimental realism
of lilies drooling from the maws of cows,
—on this I was condemned to gaze at meals
until the market for such drivel rises.
Oh, life with him was fun, such fun! Children
growing up with a zombie father, he scarcely
noticed they were there. I felt myself
a widow with three kids and a stranger boarding
who came home sometimes for meals. And yet
there once was something. . . . How naïve
I was then, just a girl, impressed by his
swagger, that cocky self-assurance he
bulged with, since the whole world was his oyster.
So destined to succeed by his own measure,
so handsome, so intent on sweeping me
off my feet—I mistook it all for love,
didn't see that I was just a trophy
among the triumphs his ticker tape recorded.
I threw my life away. Years, years
of living in the same house with nothing,

nothing to say to one another, nothing.
A man untouched by life, uncultured, his mind
a void except for business and the Market—
where would he have had the first idea
of how to find or keep another woman?

26

Now he complains that Kimberton complains, Where's the human
content in your art? That doesn't stop him, though—the clos-
ets's bursting with those crazy canvases like squares of pave-
ment somebody dropped a jar of spaghetti sauce on from a four-
teenth-story window. Today we learn that landlords like this stuff
even less than dealers, and with the rent three months behind
he'll be put out on the street come Tuesday.

And where do I fit in, in this? He'd smother me in sweet talk if I'd
give him half a chance, he's still so hot to bed me down I've got
to wrestle him when I take a shower. So why won't he let me
model for him any more? Besides, we can't eat sweet talk or the
unsold 'representations of pure emotion.'

And now that it's all over, what was in it for me besides his being so
great in bed? Well, that's not quite fair. I really liked to go to
Kimberton's, or the Museum that time he had his show, and
mingle with the viewers, dressed and made up so that none
would guess I was the model.

Didn't I get a charge from those rich old geezers drooling over me
there on the wall, standing naked as a jaybird with one foot on
the edge of Susanna's tub—not that we ever had a bathtub, I'd
have my foot poised just so on an empty box and stand there
on one leg for hours.

Or lie on the couch with a shawl half thrown around me, the fringe
covering part of my belly and one shoulder, as though while
lying there it couldn't cross my mind that any old men would
stand in line to scan my tits and get that dreamy look while their
gimlet gaze played over my bush. Art lovers all, with knowing
comments on palette, perspective, brushwork, while in their
minds they had me hanging in their smoking rooms.

And the women, looking at my body—how that made them nervous and uneasy, their bright sharp chatter about the idealization of the artist, while comparing their own flab or scrawniness to those actual portraits of my figure, my throat, my shoulders, elbows, wrists. My bubs and waist, my hips, my thighs. I guess I loved it, really, though it meant staying in this sleazy studio and cooking on an old two-burner laundry stove. Which by Tuesday he won't have.

I think by then he won't have me. I'm not one to starve for his art of pure emotion. That nude of Vladimir's is still unsold in Carstairs' window—knew she wouldn't sell, the model's such a broomstick. What Vladimir needs is a new, plump model, and he'll be about to make his mark.

Besides, he's a sweet guy and his studio has a real bedroom, and a tub and kitchen range.

27

Each breath I draw remembers
the failing of his breath.
He can't be gone forever.
I wake from sleep, or death,
where my arms again have cradled
his dear head on my breast,
I feel the pulse in his pulse beat
as though my pulse would burst.
I dread to open my eyelids,
I fear the loss the light
pitilessly shines upon.
How remorseless is the knowing
my little son is gone.
His untouched room's the sepulchre
of my future. Now I live
only to dream he's wakened.
Awake, I am alone;
my grief, a shell of stone.

One day he's playing stickball, home from school,
that night the sudden fever, higher, higher
the fever shriveling his flesh as though fire
lashed him, breathing labored, more labored, while they
with damp washcloths, wet towels, water glass with straw
are helpless, helpless. The doctor helpless. All over
so fast, playing, playing stickball and only
four days later—the nights, interminable—
only four days later, gone. Now
how can he bear to sit in his easy chair with the evening paper,
his hands full of the world's disruptions and the sports when
his son, their boy, who should be sleeping in the next room,
is gone? How can she cook a dinner in the kitchen where she poured
glasses of water he couldn't suck up through his straw?
The future withers in their minds as
they sit at the table dawdling
over coffee in silence to postpone returning
to an empty home. The waitress senses
something wrong and deeply sad, discreetly
stands at the other end of the nearly empty restaurant. This late,
one other diner only, by the kitchen door—his eye
on the mural he's been painting for his meals,
a scene, 'Il Ponte Vecchio,' he has enlarged
a hundred times from a picture postcard, giving
Ristorante di Firenze a touch
of atmosphere. He's sketched the scene
on the blank wall, tomorrow he'll put in
the colors, but now he looks at her, while
she pours him another coffee, as though
for the first time noticing her long
golden hair, slim shoulders, tapering legs,
and that look, mysterious,
on her muted, luminous features, not a smile
but an arresting trace of tragic knowledge, of one
who has already suffered a loss beyond telling,

a nameless woe
that gives her youthfulness a poignant glow—when he's done
this damned hack mural maybe he can get her
to pose, though he hasn't a nickel to pay her,
if she'd pose he could evoke that sad, luminous,
muted beauty impressionistically, now wishing
that dull couple over there would drink up and push off
so he and she can get acquainted
before she goes off duty.

Sometimes I can almost get through the day
without feeling it, without remembering,
but it's maybe when I'm pouring coffee, the black flood in a rush
from the spout as it swirls like blood in the empty white cup
and the emptiness drains out of me. I feel my veins
filling with nothing, my womb chills, and yearns,
and I feel so faint I can scarcely stand with the pot in my hand,
my head's light with streaks, specks in my eyes, I can't speak, I'm
   trying
to rise from the bed, reaching toward the doctor, pleading
'Let me hold my baby!' and there is no
baby. Then I have to walk back to the kitchen
as though nothing had happened to get the sugar and cream
and I've never seen my baby. The hollow feeling
in the pit of my stomach, it's like a stone fell
leaving nothing but the way the weight of it
was there, and then not there. When he ran off
with Janeen I felt nothing, it was like
I was so numb already there was nothing
more I could feel. Like my arms and legs are straws, my body
emptied into the light and I'm pleading, clutching
armfuls of air, the doctor jabbing my thighs with
needles, his voice coming at me from farther
and farther away, the stupor blanketing me until
I'm listening, listening in a dark silence for the sound
of the baby's first cry when he holds it up and spanks it, hearing
the echo of nothing. Just a moment, sir,
I'll pour you another cup.

Comparing the uses of carved masks found
in cognate cultures with hieroglyphs incised
on cavern walls and decipherment of scripts
from burial urns, my study proposes
how this handful of half-naked folk, who crouched
around their flickering hearths, in rituals
accepted death for both the dead and living:
When a member of the Cromlech village dies
a shaman in a mask calls up the spirits
of his ancestors and, in a trance, replies
in guttural chants to the falsetto voice
in which their queries speak through him. Thus, witnessed
by the village, may the Dead Ones be prepared
to receive their guest newborn in Death's dark cave.
Then the shaman dances praises of those deeds
left to our world's memories when he must go
where the Fathers and the Mothers wait for him.

31

He wants these signed, does he? Well then, you'd better read me what they say, my dear, my eyes aren't what they once were—this tiny type looks all a blur of wiggly lines. You typed it yourself? Ah, no offense to your typing, young lady, it's just that at my age the eyes play tricks, and the first rule of business is, *Read the fine print before you sign!* So tell me, what does it say?

. . . this one's the dissolution of the Hercules contract, is it? Good, And that's an agreement with Archimedes to take over their shares at par . . . Well, my son seems to have learned a trick or two from his old father. Now where's the spaces for my signature? There you are, all signed.

Doing business again makes me feel twenty years younger. Tell me, how's my old friend Miss Prill in the office? Not in the office anymore? And what do you do there? His secretary? Well, well. You tell your boss his father says he is to send you here two or three times a week, at the least—whether he's got papers needing my signature or not. I don't get to see many pretty girls anymore, up here in this room, at this window. Did you like the kimono?

I'm sorry, guess I'm a little confused, you remind me of someone, I thought . . . you look like somebody I used to know . . . Memory, it's memory plays tricks like that, when you get old, hiding the cards with the right names or numbers so you get mixed up. That's how you know you're growing old, when you can remember perfectly the purple dress Miss Rickaby, your teacher in the fourth grade, wore to school on Thursdays a million years ago, but you can't call back for the life of you recent names, persons you've known very well. All muddled. But I'll not forget you.

I had a daughter once, about your age . . . but that's another story . . .

And how does my son behave as your boss? You tell him, if I ever hear he's been hard on you, I'll fire him! But first, my dear, come over here, a little closer, and let me hold your hand . . . You have to get back? All right, I'll ring for Charles to see you out. But come again soon, won't you?

She reminds me . . . I can see her, there was a kimono, a Japanese kimono and she let down her hair . . . and I see her somewhere, we went to Birch Grove Park . . . someone I knew well . . . And Junior's retired Miss Prill and taken this girl in her place. Oh, oh, Charles! Charles!

32

What's this uniform? What'sa matter with you, can't read?
See, it says here on this shoulder patch, Security Guard. Yeah, I'm se-
    curity guard
at the art gallery. And I'll tell you, I gave 'em some security today.
First week on the job, and did they need security!
There he was, skulking around in the crowd that gawked at the
    window,
big show-window where they display the new paintings, see,
and what a bunch they had craning their necks out there today!
Hardly a man or boy on the avenue
but got word of what was there on show for free.
Should've seen how they shoved one another and gawked, jostled and
    argued
over who had the right to stand in front, and for how long—
What's it all about? Well, ain't I telling you? Never
did you see such a picture as that right there from the public sidewalk,
even if it is an art gallery—I mean the broad
is big as life, damned near, and she's so naked
you can see *everything,* she's standing there clasping
her tits in her hands with the nipples peeking through the fingers,
dipping her toe in a stream with a bunch of cows and a old man peep-
    ing
down on her with his gimlet eyes—you can bet
there was never less than thirty gimlets gazing
through the plate glass today, all day, at that tall, plump, naked dame,
when this guy I seen skulking for nearly an hour
at the edge of the crowd catches sight of the boss and he runs over
    shouting
'Carstairs!' he says, 'Take that picture down!
That's my painting, Carstairs! Take it down!' and Mr. Carstairs
looks right through him and says in a voice as cool as ice cream,
'I beg your pardon, sir, this painting belongs to Carstairs Gallery
and we offer it for sale.' This guy, he's not much of a specimen,
shoes all scuffed and needing heels, dirty old sweater and paint-stained
    pants,

he's shouting 'I did that work on commission for Kimberton's years
    ago!
I painted that slut of Popov's in a style
I haven't used for years!
I will not have that represent my work!' and he's pushing past Mr.
    Carstairs
pushing his way in the back of the window with a jackknife in his
    hand!
'Take care of him, John,' says Mr. Carstairs just as I grabbed his wrist
—Which one? Well, the one with the hand with the knife in it, and
    I twisted him so hard
he drops the knife and I had him down on one knee.
Then I picked him up by the collar—
Listen, Buddy, I worked for twenty-one years in the railroad round-
    house
and I can take care of a twerp painter with one hand whether he's got
    a knife or not
—and holding him up in front of all those people
who by now are gawking at him, not his picture,
I told the sonofabitch 'Push off,
and if you know what's good for you let's see the last of your back,'
and for good luck shoved him down the gallery steps.
So I guess I gave some security pretty good today. A place like that
needs a guard. Never know who'll make trouble.

33

Another triumph! Roars of applause, three curtain calls
and even the stagehands cheering . . . Why, then,
such tossings, turnings, keyed-up fitful sleep
and another waking to the dull dead light
of 4 A.M., gathering the shreds
urgent as prophecy? Again he's just stepped back
through the curtain after the last bow, still in his tails,
walking beside a pool, a pool shaped like a tureen—
Look, she's in it, struggling, needs his help—he grasps
her wrist and pulls her safely out, her white throat
gleaming upward as her head falls back, blonde hair in a wave
across his arm, a few deft strokes of the saw and
'See, you felt nothing!' as her arm
twists free in his hand
cleanly, like the wing of a roasted chicken and the meat
is white and firm, tender, sweet and good. Her shoulder
smooth and white, she smiles to see
him stack the white bones on his plate and with her hand
leads him—in a low-cut, off-the-shoulder sheer green gown—
to the couch, gown slipping off her shoulder, hips, knees,
ankles as she flings herself on the sheeted table,
breasts flashing white and moves his hand to her hip
looking up expectantly. He knows at once
what he's to do and 'You won't feel a thing,' his clever fingers
guide the sawteeth and her shapely leg
drops off just as a well-carved turkey leg
when the knife has sliced straight through the joint
comes neatly free. Her wound is healed and sound,
yet she floods her dilate gaze on him aghast
—Why has she turned against him?—
as the growl gurgles in his gorge and his tusks gnaw
a clotted, gristled end of thigh. Her lips
freeze around a syllable from terror's source: no word
has she yet spoken, though these two have time and time
while hackles thrust like icicles upon his neck

goggled at this scene,
no word save for her throttled scream
in a voice like his that sears through sleep
trying to stop all this from happening, or trying
to tell him what he wakens not to hear.

34

Where to, Doc? Oh, I know that address, know the very house—
You're not near as pretty as my last fare I took there,
a real sweetheart. That was day before yesterday. Yesterday,
I was slowing down for this light, right here at this corner,
I hit a kid—heard him thud against my right front fender,
looked up to see him fall, seemed like under the wheel, felt
a bump. My God, I jammed the brakes, jumped
out of the cab, ran around to see what happened, take the kid
to a hospital, my heart's in my mouth. Yeah, you can bet
I felt rotten. So while I'm running
around in front of the cab, the kid's partner
leaps into the back seat, holds a knife to my fare and takes off
with his wristwatch and wallet. When he sees me coming
the kid in the street is already on his feet pushing
through the crowd on the sidewalk—a lot of help *they* were—
and runs off to find his pal. Run over? Like hell run over,
jammed a hunk of board under the wheel as he ducked to make me
    think
I'd broke his leg. Wish to hell I'd a broke his leg for real.
You can bet my fare was pretty steamed
and so was I, after we spent half the afternoon at the station
giving descriptions, looking at mug shots, not picking up any dough
    doing that either.
Between them those two little bastards got over a hundred bucks
    and a hot watch
and neither a day over thirteen. What a town. I bet
you see a lot, going around to your patients,
eh, Doc? You must go all over town. No? Nothing ever happens?
Well, you're a lucky fellow. This place
is a jungle, believe me. That's two bucks forty for this ride.

35

I saw it happen, it was horrible. The girl—she works in our of-
fice—she had just come out of the door to the building. Why
only this morning we rode up in the elevator together. When-
ever I see her I think

Wow, what a looker! When she'd walk past my desk on the way to the
cooler or the ladies' john, her body just flowed, like her wavy
dark long hair, and it would take me ten minutes to stop shaking
inside

and get myself pulled together to work at the shipping forms again.
She had just come out on the sidewalk—I was already there—
when this streetcar came clanging down the track.

She started to run for it, she ran along the sidewalk on her toes, her
little high heels making a *clacka clacka clacka* sound on the con-
crete as she ran with her arms stretched out at her sides—

girls never know how to run. By the time she got to the corner the
people had piled out the rear door, pushing each other down as
they came, and the boarders up front were shoving inside, you
could hear their coins clink in the fare box.

The front door closed as she pushed her hand against it. She'd been
all set to climb aboard, her head was pitched forward toward the
door, when the car gave a sudden lurch and the handbar—

the bar on the side of the door you can hold onto while getting into
the car—it juts out a little, and it smashed into the side of her
head. My God, she went down and the back of her head hit
the cobbles. I could see

blood oozing out of her nose and mouth and soaking her hair. I
looked up and caught sight of this doctor getting out of a taxi
halfway along the block—saw his black bag—and ran

calling *Doctor!* though already I knew there was nothing he could
do. The girls say she lived with her mother who dotes on her
night and day since her sister ran off with a vaudeville magician
last year. When I got to the doctor I said,

Doctor, there's been a terrible accident in the next block, and I got
it all out without wheezing. The trolley took off like the driver
never knew what he'd done. Her name was Wilma. Wilma.

Wilma.

36

The Lord's judgment took the child, the baby
born dead. From the minute she laid eyes on
that sharper and stole off with him, to stand
in the spotlight in plain view on stage
she was flaunting her sin in the eyes of the Lord.
And now he's of course abandoned her, run off
with some other Dumb Dora just as big a fool
as she was, leaving her with nothing, nothing
but the memory of those months of nights
in fleabag hotels and her with this judgment
growing in her belly till at last
in a rented room, her screaming with the pain
and the doctor getting there too late to save
the poor little tyke. She never saw him,
there was something strange about the way
he shot her full of sedatives *after* the birth
and wrapped the poor little thing in a towel
and by the time she came around it was gone.
And so was he. It's the Lord's judgment on her.
She won't come home to her mother, though her heart
is breaking, so stubborn she is she'd rather die
in the street than admit that I was right and she
was wrong. And I'm left here to grieve alone,
a woman of forty-two, with no daughters,
left to grieve for her and for poor Wilma
struck down by a judgment of the Lord,
a sentence passed, twenty years late, on me.
Oh, he was handsome, rich, so generous,
those ten-dollar tips night after night,
when he grabbed my wrist in the restaurant and whispered
he'd show me a time, oh, I knew it was wrong, but was it
too bad to let him fix me in a nice apartment
where he'd spend the night whenever he'd pull the wool
over his wife? I still remember the feel
of his worsted jacket, the silk of the shirts he wore,

remember the pattern on the first dress he gave me,
and the swish around my knees of that kimono.
How I'd put that on after hanging my slip in the bathroom
and while he waited on the bed, let down my hair
and come to him. And he'd be waiting there, reading
the papers from that pigskin case he always carried,
marking *Barron's,* figuring his next deal, making
money in his head—could I believe my luck!—until
when he'd hear me open the door he'd sweep it
all into the case and shove it under the bed. He'd say,
as I slipped off the kimono, how I looked like Venus
in some old painting—Oh, but he had a sweet mouth—
and how my loving him made him become
some pagan God. I knew how wrong it was, but that
just made me the more excited. He must be
getting on an old man now. I thought I'd never
forgive his walking out that morning, leaving
just that envelope with ten hundred-dollar bills.
What good was I to him then, with a
child coming on and him wanting only
the good time, not a family in shame? He never
even saw her at all.

                No need to tell
Eileen, a sister knows. More a trial
than a blessing her life long, her Johnny is,
but I forgive him all he's done to her,
for that very week didn't he bring home to dinner
William, and he'd only just met him, new at the roundhouse.
Thank God I didn't show yet, and Willy proposed
a fortnight after. If he ever did suspect
why Wilma was born so soon he didn't let on,
poor man. I named her after him. And now
struck down with her whole life before her—
It's the Lord's judgment took the child.

37

You know the boss has noticed you—how well you handled
that Apical shipment when Jack was out sick, he's noticed
that for the past six months your tallies have tallied
exactly, best records kept in Record Keeping, and you've never
been late to work. So it's about time
you got a raise, right? Been at the job how long now?
You mutter to yourself walking to the bus, thinking
maybe the boss doesn't have his mind on your promotion
because his mind may be on his old dad slowly dying
in an armchair, with a butler watching for him to twitch or wiggle
a finger to show he wants a drink of water or something. It's
that bad, they say. Been that bad for months, now—Wilma,
poor Wilma's the only one who ever went to the old man's house,
bringing him papers to sign. Said he could barely
hold the pen yet grabbed her wrist and tried to run his hand all over
   her
like he thought she was somebody else. She got a good look
around inside the house, with woven hangings
on the walls where there weren't paintings, and
what paintings! Remember how she blushed, telling the girls of
nudes, stark-naked women bathing, pools with naked women,
pools with cows. Wouldn't you think
a man that rich would have a taste for something not
so obvious? Every time you think of
Wilma, you see a sort of double-take, Wilma
sashaying past your desk and you can't tear your eyes
from her curved shoulders, breasts, curved hips and her long
dark wavy hair, and she's lying there
with the blood oozing out of her nose, her mouth, the cobbles
stained with her blood—it's been months now,
you can't forget. It hurts to think
you never actually *spoke* to her, you never
could get your goddamned breath, keep it from
strangling your voice just when you're about to speak. Same
thing in the office. You can keep the most accurate

records in Record Keeping, handle the biggest
shipments of the year to Summit, to Paragon, but
with a promotion you'd have to speak
all the time to the women, and the boss,
he's noticed you.

38

Dear Sis,
         Don't tear this up before you read it.
Soon as I'd told you why I'd called, I knew
you'd hang up—but Sis, you've got to let me tell you
why I need you here. He fired Charles
a month ago. Since then we've had three women,
live-ins, to cook, and bathe and dress and nurse him,
tend his every whim. The first two lasted
almost a week apiece. He drove them crazy
with his irascible demands. When the third one dropped
her heavy shopping bag, our family silver
tumbled down the stairs. Where could I hire
an honest woman with an angel's patience
in a town like this? There's no one now
but him and me. He's fading fast, and I,
I'm desperate. That's what I've got to tell you.
You remember how he was, impatient,
so intolerant of anyone else's least
incompetence? This morning, I sat and watched him
fumble with his belt tongue, trying to thread it
through his trouser loops. For twenty minutes
he sits there fumbling, doesn't know I'm here,
fumbling in a somewhere lost in time,
helpless. He's out of it for hours on end,
then snaps back, imperious, demands
I do his bidding, fix his tea, or listen
while he tells me for the ninetieth time
how he worshipped Mother, how she wronged him,
or else it's you he's calling, thinks you're here,
calls and calls you, sometimes in his mind
confusing you with Aunt Millie, or talks about
the silk kimono—he gave you a kimono?—
thinking of you. Then back he goes to Mother,
how bitter she's made all his life, her scorn
singeing his satisfactions. I hear this

while setting him up in bed, while bathing him,
dressing, feeding, pouring out his dose
of medicine. He's helpless as a babe
and I'm the father of my baby father
who's old and sick and shrunken, cannot walk:
a decrepit baby who will never grow
into a strong and healthy boy.
                                  Last night
he drifted back to consciousness—he sleeps
at all odd hours—wakes up at 3 A.M.
chipper as a lad, starts reminiscing
about our visits with Billy Hoop.
You never knew him and his slattern wife,
Indians, they were; I was the only boy
in my whole class who'd met a real Indian.
I'd come along on Sunday morning visits.
Had rows of corn and beanpoles in their yard.

He never worked, but from his chair received
our father on his porch. Playing near
the stoop while they talked business, I could hear—
No stock but was a bull. Why, Dad believed
all of his tips because, when Billy braved
those shells in no-man's-land and the sniper's fire
to drag a doughboy back from the barbed wire,
it would be a Senior Partner that he'd saved
—a loan of life, still, after a decade
amortized by calls that named the share
certain to rise, and an instant fortune made.
But who owed Dad the debt that Billy's words
were to redeem? Why should his tipster care
that all our fairy gold would turn to turds?

Dad's eyes shine with an autumnal light
remembering how Mrs. Hoop would hand me
a glass of cider, cookies as big as saucers.
Then he's on about the deals he made
or nearly made decades ago—Fitzhugh,
that sozzled engineer across the street

whose wife, a lush, had a silver cocktail shaker,
Art Deco, always half full on their bar,
How Fitz and he had this scheme to corner copper,
all the copper rights in Venezuela,
for Fitz spent years there, Fitz had built the mines,
and all the men who count in Venezuela
are Fitz's friends. They tell him what's going on.
Fitz knows just when they'll throw those generals out
and won't we cash in then. He talks as though
I'm Fitz and the dream's about to happen,
then suddenly his face goes hard, his mouth
tightens, a slipknot, and the gloom of the real
darkens his mind. But if you wonder why
I'm telling this to you, you ought to know
it's you he calls, it's you he want to talk to,
wants to have beside him, now he knows
he's dying. This is how it's ending: sad,
sad, half helpless, no dignity is left him,
no joy. No use to cable Bud COME HOME,
he's deep in his dig and by the time he'd get here
—if he would—he'd be too late. I never knew
what came between you, whatever it was he did or
what you thought he'd done, none of my business,
but isn't this the time to let it be?
Bygones are past, whatever the injuries,
time to forgive them, while he's still alive.
Can't you spell me for a day or two
and let the old man die in peace? It's not
just him you've turned your back on, Sis. I need
help. I can't take it any more. That's
what I'm saying: Help. Help, Sis, I'm saying *Help*.

39

A week after the interment
—at which, by his father's express desire,
no one was present but himself—he started
sifting through the deeds, correspondence, records of purchases and
        sales of securities and bonds,
the letters on stationery bearing the quadrupled names of law firms,
        brokerage houses, accountancy partnerships.
In the top two file drawers these were arranged by subject and
        filed by dates in folders,
but the middle drawers offered a chaos of recent vintage,
letters and drafts of letters in a senseless jumble.
Yet these must be sorted out to determine
whether there were valid claims against the estate, or,
contrariwise, if the estate had assets
otherwise unrecorded.

The bottom drawer was stuck.

He pulled and wrenched the handle,
but nothing would dislodge it.
At last, with screwdriver and hammer, he managed to pry it loose.
    Within,
a steel box
secured by a large padlock
hanging on a hasp.
Neither in this drawer nor in his father's desk could he find a key
to fit this lock.

Nothing to do but cut the hasp with a hacksaw.
After an hour and a half, sweating under the lights,
at last he had eked the blade twice through the hasp
—it was only half the thickness of the lock.
The hinged boxtop
flung open:
heaps of faded photographs, old envelopes

addressed to his father and stamped with 2¢ stamps,
and a thick packet of legal papers in blue covers to which were stuck
the disintegrated bits of rubber bands.

Father as a skinny freckled kid, in baseball uniform
—peaked cap, striped wool shirt and knickers,
a fielder's mitt holding his fist. Father
in a canoe, squinting into the Brownie
held by invisible hands on shore.

And who is this flapper in a cloche? Why look,
it's Mother as a girl,
the girl his father stands beside in this one,
stands in his wing collar and in his hands a bowler hat,
his eyes determinedly staring into the Graflex
while the photographer, beneath his black sheet, squeezes the shutter
—that was forty years ago. And still
his father stares, and Mother,
with her legs demurely crossed and white shoes
pointing downward as she sits in the wicker armchair beside him,
looks toward her toes with a faint smile.

Here they are, at an amusement park.
Here, they're feeding a caged bear.
Who took this one, he wonders?
And here, their wedding photographs, enlarged and mounted
on stippled cardboard folders. What were they thinking,
that day?

The thick folded dockets in blue covers bearing
the triple-decker names of their respective firms of attorneys-at-law,
the sordid accusations, the nitpicking accounting
of how much each gave, how little got,
from his soured investments, their mutual recriminations, years of
        fighting, wrangling,
half-hearted conciliations,
renewed hostilities.

the misery, in the house, filled with epergnes and paintings and
antique chairs the children mustn't sit on,

of his blighted childhood. Photos
of himself in sailor suit, of Bud
in his kiddie-car, and Sis
dressed as a butterfly for her rhythmic-dancing class recital,
and there they are together,
skinny-limbed in swimsuits
on the banks of Buglers Pond.
Sis would laugh at that one.

She hasn't been in this house
in over fifteen years, and won't return
even now that it's all over.
Here's another envelope, sealed—more photos
—some woman he's never seen, young and flirty,
looks like taken at a booth on a boardwalk,
from her clothes and hairdo, twenty years ago.
A real looker.
Hasn't he seen that face somewhere? An uncanny
tingle runs across him as he sees
she reminds him of . . . Wilma . . . a lot like Wilma. . . .
But all that means is, like father, like son,
both drawn to the same type. So that was it,
in a sealed envelope. Dad.
was it all over this piece of cake, losing
everybody's love—was it worth it?

40

For their girls the oncome of the menses is
a time of much gravity, much joy. When blood
first appears the girl is quickly sequestered
in a tree-house, attended only by crones
—not, as with the Kumiak, because unclean,
but to give her spirit place to meditate
and grow into her woman's body. A week
usually suffices, the spirit's growth
fully attained by the end of menstrual flow.
The women chant, encircling the tree, *Girl-child*
climbed up into the sky-house, comes down Woman!
Now the little girls cluster by her, singing,
weaving plaits of flowers in her braided hair,
now her mother lies upon a litter bed
and now she climbs through her mother's legs again
to symbolize her second birth as woman.
By that night's fire her father chants her dower.

41

She always piled her things
neatly on the chair,
pleated skirt across the back,
middy blouse, the slip
and now the bra
laid on the seat. Next
she'd unhook her garter belt,
step out of her shoes, slide
the stockings down her legs
and put them, rolled, inside
the shoes beneath the chair.
But now she stood there, tilting
a little forward, for
as she leaned to arrange the blouse
she'd caught a glimpse of her own
hip's curve in the pier glass,
and once again drew herself up
to regard her full-length image.
From inside the walnut frame
a pearly-fleshed young woman
gazed at her. Not long before
her body had been chubby
but suddenly had grown in strange
ways, blubbery fat falling
away as she lengthened, and now
these rosy-nippled breasts stuck out,
wagging a little if she unexpectedly
turned, or when she bent down after
freeing them from the bra,
hanging like weights of a clock.
And her hips were broader, thighs
more slender. All these changes
and the curse. How gross
even to think, how disgusting,

a Kotex clipped to an elastic belt
and walk like a waddling duck for days
while her head ached and stomach cramped
and the icky blood oozed
out of her. What was growing up,
being a woman, that required such weird
things of a girl? But now the tap
was running, steam rising from the huge
clawfooted tub, and as she looked
again into the pier glass
over the shoulder of her glowing
reflection she caught a glint
on the transom above the door—
A little shudder ran through her,
the inexplicable notion that there was someone
watching. She knew nobody else was home
just now, nevertheless her skin
tingled with the expectation of being
watched by nearly unseen eyes that peered
through the tilted transom. She remembered,
when her folks moved in last week
Clara, downstairs, told her this whole building
had been the house of a rich old miser
who kept pictures of naked women
bathing on all the walls,
and maybe he had hidden, upstairs,
like Bluebeard, the women on whose baths
he spied and to whom he did
unspeakable things behind locked doors.
What if the mirror held its images
after a person moved away from the glass?
—suppose she in her own nakedness
appeared to someone else looking
into the glass at some later time,
or, if while she peered into it,
the shape would appear of some woman
long ago, preparing to bathe as she
herself was doing, the leering image
of the old lecher gazing down on her

as she bent over to take off
a shoe. From downstairs and upstairs
came teeming sounds of the families
in the other apartments. Her nipples
had got hard as raisins, pulling
the skin of her ruddy paps. Now she tossed
her head to rid her mind of
fantastic thoughts and lifted
her foot across the high side
of the tub. In another moment
she was floating on her back in a steaming
pool, soaping her arms and thighs
with a fat sponge, feeling the warmth
of the water caress the tender parts
beneath the patch of hair that shaded
her crotch. She purred a little,
lazily lolling in the enamelled bowl
that encircled her
with the warm, warm water.

42

Father dead and buried, the old house sold—
he's free, now free of everything that dragged him down.
His depression, he came at last to understand,
was caused by his long failure
to honor his ancestors. Overcome
by this inescapable guilt when he thought of
his father's fathers, of his own
late father, of how they had quarrelled and how
little he knew of either his father's feelings
or of his own past, he
booked flight for a return
to the homeland his forebears had fled from
and four generations never had seen. On arrival,
wherever he went, scenes strangely excited him: peasants
beneath a sodden sky digging rutabagas with clumsy hoes;
women, heads tied up in ragged shawls, bearing
meager parcels in bags of knotted string
as they trudge through mud toward leaky farmhouses; and men
in fur hats who step down from the rattletrap bus
that once a day runs through the village. Standing
before the one café, he sees
just such a man get off the bus—a man
exactly like the photo his father
once had shown him of his own great-
great-grandfather! The same
fur hat, the same round spectacles, same mouth
tightly clenched above an identical beard. A great
flood of emotion—impulsively he rushes
forward, flings his arms
around the stranger, burying his head
on the man's shoulder and cries
'Grandfather!
Forgive me!' Then, getting a grip on himself,
he backs away, smiling,
opens the door of his rented car and

drives off unembarrassed,
more secure now in his deepened knowledge
of his past.
                    As his car sped off
between rows of leafless trees,
glancing at his rearview mirror for one last look
at the double of his ancestor,
he sees two men in uniform crossing the square,
then the road turned and he lost
their tiny image as they said
'We always knew you are an enemy
of the Fatherland,' confronting
the bearded man in fur hat (a tailor
who had lived all his life in this village).
'Tell us: What did the foreign stranger say to you?' In vain
he protests, he doesn't know—he
understands no language but their own. 'We have
devices in the barracks basement that can restore
memory of other tongues. . . . There must
have been *some* reason why the foreign agent
arrives in this village, waits half the morning for the bus,
and then confides his message
to you and you alone.' Expressionless,
he walks across the square between them
like a man who knows exactly
where he is going and what
is the shape of the future.

43

That's it!—the final entry on my list: Shards,
flutes, axheads, hollow pointed bones (awls, or pens
to write prayers, laws, accounts, love messages
of which we've found no trace) . . . What I can't resist
is the evidentiary search, when mind
and intuition are accomplices, as
in the solution of a crime. Look, more clues
than I'll ever use, yet who could get enough
evidence to verify what inference
grasps as the only truth? Based on these found things
spared the depredations of decay or time,
my study of a culture at a distance
must, so little known of its inner life, be
fiction. And now, look into my notes, and write.